Thank you to the generous team who gave their time and talents to make this book possible:

Author
Jane Kurtz

Illustrator
April Philips

Creative directors
Caroline Kurtz, Jane Kurtz, and Kenny Rasmussen

Translator
Worku L. Mulat

Designer
Beth Crow

Ready Set Go Books, an Open Hearts Big Dreams Project

Special thanks to Ethiopia Reads donors and staff for
believing in this project and helping get it started-- and
for arranging printing, distribution, and training in Ethiopia.

Printed in the United States of America

02/09/19

Only in Ethiopia

በኢትዮጵያ ብቻ

English and Amharic

High in a mountain
cloud forest, the
black lion yawns.

በዳመና ከተከበበው
ተራራማ ጫካ ውስጥ
ጥቁሩ አንበሳ ያዛጋል።

Only in Ethiopia. Nowhere else.
በኢትዮጵያ እንጅ በሌላ
አገር አይገኝም።

Low on the Afar plains,
the Somali wild donkey
kicks and grazes.

በአፋር ዝቅተኛ ቦታዎች የሜዳ
አህዮች ሳር እየጋጡ ይራገጣሉ።

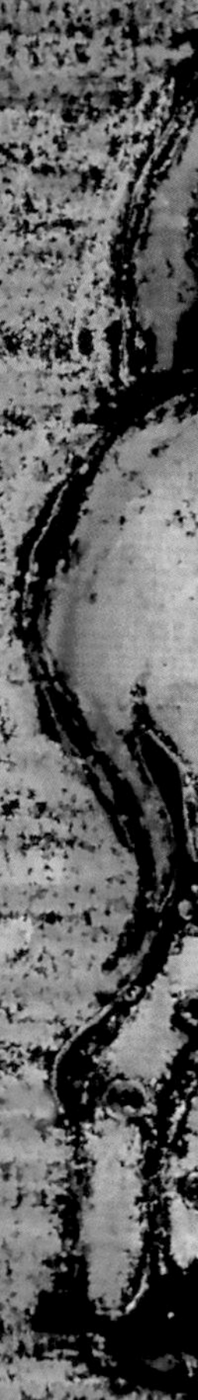

Only in Ethiopia.

ኢትዮጵያ
ውስጥ ብቻ።

High on a branch,
the Bale mountain
vervet carries and
protects her baby.

ከፍ ብሎ በሚገኙት የዛፎች
ቅርንጫፍ ላይ የባሌ
ተራራ ጦጣ ልጇን አዝላ
ትንከባከባለች፤ ይንከባከባሉ።

Only in Ethiopia.

ኢትዮጵያ
ውስጥ ብቻ።

Low in the white
heather, the Ethiopian
wolf hunts grass rats.

በረባዳው የነጭ ሣር ሜዳ ላይ
የኢትዮጵያ ቀበሮዎች የሣር
አይጦችን ያድናሉ።

Only in Ethiopia.

ኢትዮጵያ ውስጥ ብቻ።

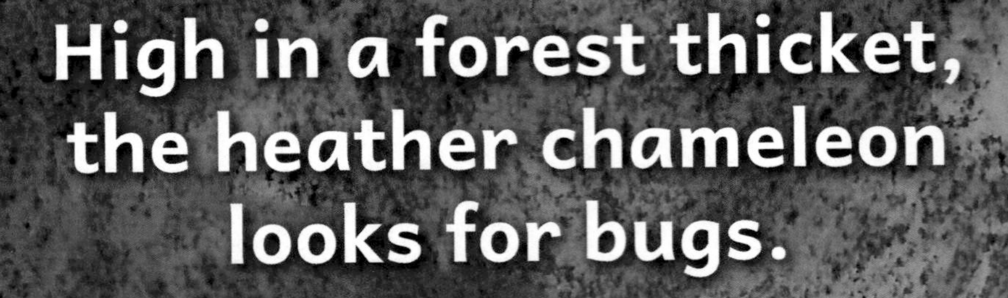

High in a forest thicket,
the heather chameleon
looks for bugs.

ከፍ ብሎም በዛፎች
ላይ እስስቶች ጥቃቅን
ነፍሳትን ያድናሉ።

Only in Ethiopia.

ኢትዮጵያ ውስጥ ብቻ።

Low in a pile of plants,
the Bale Mountains
tree frog hides.

የባሌን ተራራ ግርጌ በሸፈኑት
እጽዋቶች ውስጥ የባሌ
ተራራ የዛፍ እንቁራሪቶች
ተደብቀዋል።

Only in Ethiopia.

ኢትዮጵያ ውስጥ ብቻ።

High in the mountains, the mountain Nyala listens with its large ears.

ከፍ ብሎ በተራራው ዐለቶች ላይ የተራራ ኒያላ ጆሮዎቹን አቁሞ ያዳምጣል።

Only in Ethiopia.

ኢትዮጵያ ውስጥ ብቻ።

Low in the dirt, the
big-headed mole rat
digs a tunnel to its food.

ዝቅ ብሎም በአቧራማው በረሃ
ፍልፈል ምግብ ለማግኘት
መሬት ይቆፍራል።

Only in Ethiopia.

ኢትዮጵያ
ውስጥ ብቻ።

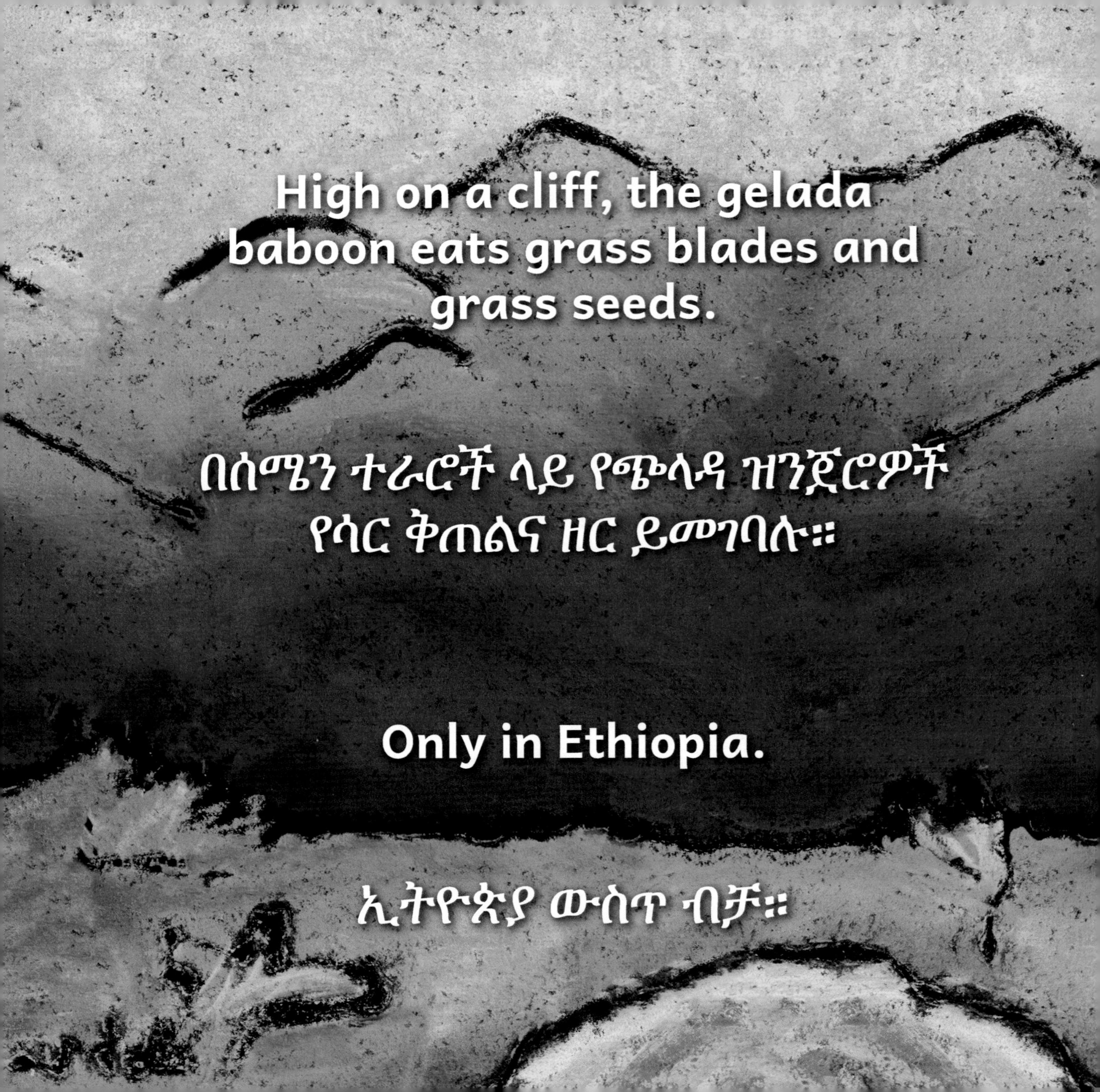

High on a cliff, the gelada baboon eats grass blades and grass seeds.

በሰሜን ተራሮች ላይ የጬላዳ ዝንጀሮዎች
የሳር ቅጠልና ዘር ይመገባሉ።

Only in Ethiopia.

ኢትዮጵያ ውስጥ ብቻ።

Low in a field, the yellow fronted parrot spots seeds to eat.

ዝቅ ብሎ በሚገኘው መስክ ባለቢጫ ግንባሯ በቀቀን ዘርን ትለቅማለች።

Only in Ethiopia.
ኢትዮጵያ ውስጥ ብቻ።

High in the sky the
Prince Ruspolis turaco
flashes its red wings.
በጣም ከፍ ብሎ በሚገኘው
ሰማይ ላይ ሩስፖሊስ ቴራኮ
ወፍ ቀይ ክንፎቹን እያማታ
ይበራል።

Only in Ethiopia.

ኢትዮጵያ ውስጥ ብቻ።

Many animals make life interesting and beautiful all around the world.

ብዙ እንስሳት በዓለም ዙሪያ ሕይወትን አስደሳችና ያማረች አድርገዋታል።

But some animals are treasures,
found only in Ethiopia.

የተወሰኑ እንስሳት ግን በኢትዮጵያ ብቻ
የሚገኙ ድንቅ ሀብቶች ናቸው።

About The Story

High in the mountains, nyala climb. They live in Ethiopia and nowhere else. Yes, Ethiopia has more than 30 mammal species that are endemic, meaning the animals occur naturally only in that country. Here are fun facts about a few of the animals in this book. You can spot an image of the mountain nyala on the Ethiopian ten cent coin. But you may never see the shy animal that mostly navigates at night and feeds where anyone approaching will send a warning by stepping on twigs. With their large ears, they hear and seem to melt mysteriously away. Gelada baboons sleep on cliff ledges and forage for food in grasslands so high in the mountains that the baboons sometimes experience frost and depend on long, heavy capes of hair to keep themselves warm. They are the only primates that primarily eat grass blades and seeds.

Big-headed African mole-rats mostly forage above ground, digging a new tunnel to a patch of plants where they can eat for about 20 minutes and then retreat, blocking the tunnel from the inside. They have become expert tunnel diggers to avoid their predators, especially the Ethiopian wolf, which eats mostly mole-rats. Prince Ruspoli was an Italian aristocrat and explorer who traveled to Ethiopia in the 1890s to gather new species for scientific study. Unfortunately, he got in the way of an elephant and died on the trip. The colorful bird with its long tail, found in his collecting bag, was named after him.

https://www.theguardian.com/environment/2011/nov/20/birdwatch-ethio-pia-feather-species

These days, rare black lions can be found only in remote small pockets of Ethiopia—such as Bale National Park. (https://news.nationalgeographic.com/2017/02/black-mane-ethiopian-lions-video-endangered-species/) “There were lions everywhere in Ethiopia, but their habitat is shrinking,” says Zelealem Tefera, country head of the Born Free Foundation, a conservation group. What can you discover about the other birds, mammals and reptiles that are endemic to Ethiopia?

About Bale National Park

Located in the Bale Mountains, Bale Mountain National Park is home to many animals that can be found only in Ethiopia. The park has been named to the UNESCO World Heritage Tentative List because of its amazing variety of landscapes This undulating landscape includes lakes and swamps, grassy meadows, forests, and volcanic mountain peaks.

Bale Mountain Lodge is an example of one effort to save some of the endangered species that live in the park. Agriculture and grazing from goats and cows and sheep destroy habitat that the wild animals desperately need to survive. Tourists and the money they bring into the area can help provide other ways for people to make a living and also support the Ethiopian wildlife authorities in their efforts to save these species that are found in no other country on Earth.

https://www.awf.org/projects/bale-mountain-lodge

About the Author

Jane Kurtz learned to read in Maji, Ethiopia. Many years later, she helped start the not-for-profit Ethiopia Reads, hoping to share book love with young readers in Ethiopia and her own Ethiopian-American grandchildren.

She has published almost forty books for young readers and is on the faculty of the Vermont College of Fine Arts MFA in Children's and Young Adult Literature.

Jane has volunteered with Ethiopia Reads for almost twenty years and now is part of the team creating Ready Set Go Books

About the Illustrator

April Philips' lifelong love for art, both classic and modern, was handed down from her uniquely talented mother. Taking that inspiration, April hopes to inspire another generations' love of art with her book illustrations and teaching.

About Ready Set Go Books

Reading has the power to change lives, but many children and adults in Ethiopia cannot read. One reason is that Ethiopia has very few books in local languages to give people a chance to practice reading. Ready Set Go books wants to close that gap and open a world of ideas and possibilities for kids and their communities.

When you buy a Ready Set Go book, you provide critical funding to create and distribute more books.

Learn more at: http://openheartsbigdreams.org/book-project/

Ready Set Go 10 Books

In 2018, Ready Set Go Books decided to experiment by trying a few new books in larger sizes.

Sometimes it was the art that needed a little more room to really shine. Sometimes the story or nonfiction text was a bit more complicated than the short and simple text used in most of our current early reader books.

We are calling these our “Ready Set Go 10” books as a way to show these ones are bigger and also sometimes have more words on the page. We are happy to hear feed-back on these new books and on all our books.

About Open Hearts Big Dreams

Open Hearts Big Dreams began as a volunteer organization, led by **Ellenore Angelidis** in Seattle, Washington, to provide sustainable funding and strategic support to Ethiopia reads, collaborating with **Jane Kurtz**. OHBD has now grown to be its own nonprofit organization supporting literacy, art, and technology for young people in Ethiopia.

Ellenore comes from a family of teachers who believe education is a human right, and opportunity should not depend on your birthplace. And as the adoptive mother of a little girl who was born in Ethiopia and learned to read in the U.S., as well as an aspiring author, she finds the chance to positively impact literacy hugely compelling!

About the Language

Amharic is a Semetic language -- in fact, the world's second-most widely spoken Semetic language, after Arabic. Starting in the 12th century, it became the Ethiopian language that was used in official transactions and schools and became widely spoken all over Ethiopia. It's written with its own characters, over 260 of them. Eritrea and Ethiopia share this alphabet, and they are the only countries in Africa to develop a writing system centuries ago that is still in use today!

About the Translation

Worku L. Mulat joined the translation team of Ready Set Go Books early in 2019. He holds a PhD from University College Cork in Ireland, an MSc from Gent University, Belgium, and a BSc from Asmara University, Eritrea. Dr. Worku has published extensively professional articles on high impact journals such as Malaria Journal, Environmental Monitoring and Assessment, Ecological Indicators, Bioresource Technology, and PLOS ONE. He also co-authored three books with a main theme of Environmental conservation. Currently he is working for Open Hearts Big Dreams Fund as Innovation Center Lead in Model projects being implemented in Ethiopia. He is also a research associate at Tree Foundation which strives to save Ethiopian Orthodox church forests.

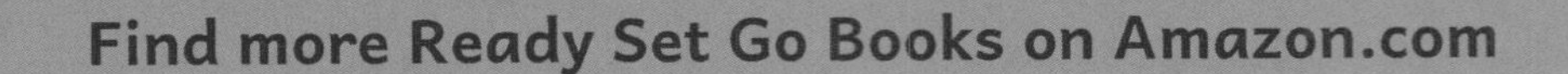

To view all available titles, search "Ready Set Go Ethiopia" or scan QR code

Chaos

Talk Talk Turtle

The Glory of Gondar

We Can Stop the Lion

Not Ready!

Fifty Lemons

Count For Me

Too Brave

Tell Me What You Hear

Made in the USA
Middletown, DE
20 May 2019